Anger Management

of related interest

Enhancing Self-Esteem
A Self-Esteem Training Package for Individuals with Disabilities
Nick Hagiliassis and Hrepsime Gulbenkoglu, published with Scope (Vic.) Ltd
ISBN 1 84310 353 2

Assessing and Developing Communication and Thinking Skills in People with Autism and Communication Difficulties
A Toolkit for Parents and Professionals
Kate Silver, Autism Initiatives
ISBN 1 84310 352 4

People with Autism Behaving Badly
Helping People with ASD Move On from Behavioral and Emotional Challenges
John Clements
ISBN 1 84310 765 1

People Skills for Young Adults
Márianna Csóti
ISBN 1 85302 716 2

Helping Adolescents and Adults to Build Self-Esteem
A Photocopiable Resource Book
Deborah Plummer
ISBN 1 84310 185 8

Relationship Development Intervention with Children, Adolescents and Adults
Social and Emotional Development Activities for Asperger Syndrome, Autism, PDD and NLD
Steven E. Gutstein and Rachelle K. Sheely
ISBN 1 84310 717 1

Drama Workshops for Anger Management and Offending Behaviour
James Thompson
ISBN 1 85302 702 2

Anger Management

An Anger Management Training Package for Individuals with Disabilities

Hrepsime Gulbenkoglu and Nick Hagiliassis

Jessica Kingsley Publishers
London and Philadelphia

First published in 2006
by Jessica Kingsley Publishers
116 Pentonville Road
London N1 9JB, UK
and
400 Market Street, Suite 400
Philadelphia, PA 19106, USA

www.jkp.com

Copyright © Scope (Vic.) Ltd 2006

Library of Congress Cataloging in Publication Data
Gulbenkoglu, Hrepsime, 1951-
 Anger management : an anger management training package for individuals with disabilities / Hrepsime Gulbenkoglu and Nick Hagiliassis.
  p. cm.
 Includes bibliographical references.
 ISBN-13: 978-1-84310-436-0 (pbk. : alk. paper)
 ISBN-10: 1-84310-436-9 (pbk. : alk. paper) 1. People with disabilities--Psychology. 2. People with mental disabilities--Psychology. 3. Anger. 4. Self-help techniques--Study and teaching. 5. Problem solving--Study and teaching. 6. Assertiveness training. I. Hagiliassis, Nick, 1970- II. Title.
 HV1568.G87 2006
 152.4'7087--dc22

                                                                        2006011507

British Library Cataloguing in Publication Data
A CIP catalogue record for this book is available from the British Library

ISBN-13: 978 1 84310 436 0
ISBN-10: 1 84310 436 9

Printed and bound in Great Britain by
Printwise (Haverhill) Ltd, Sufolk

This training package provides a starting point for running a programme to help individuals with disabilities to overcome problems with anger. While all care has been taken in the preparation of the training package, in no event shall the authors, the various collaborators, Jessica Kingsley Publishers, or Scope (Vic.) Ltd be liable for any damages or consequences resulting from direct, indirect, correct or incorrect use of this training package. It is the responsibility of the user to ensure that the training package is appropriate for the individual. This training package should *not* be used as a substitute for seeking professional diagnosis, treatment and care.

Contents

List of Hand-outs and Overheads

Introduction

Background

Research shows that many people with learning disabilities have difficulty in managing angry feelings (Hill and Bruininks 1984; Sigafoos *et al.* 1994; Smith *et al.* 1996; Taylor *et al.* 2002), and that poor anger control is an important determinant of challenging behaviour for this group (Taylor 2002, Taylor *et al.* 2002). The behavioural expressions of anger, such as verbal or physical aggression, can present as a significant personal and social barrier for people with disabilities, their families and support staff. For these reasons, there is a continued need for the development of interventions in this area.

Group-based anger management programmes are readily available to members of the general community. However, standard anger management programmes are not always accessible to people with cognitive difficulties and/or people with complex communication needs, in particular those with expressive language difficulties. For example, the heavy emphasis on the need to contribute to group processes using varying levels of verbal ability can be a barrier for people who use non-verbal or augmentative communication approaches. The few specialised anger management programmes developed to date for people with disabilities (e.g., Benson 1992) are generally targeted at individuals with mild to moderate degrees of intellectual disability, and they require further modification for people whose cognitive limitations are more severe in nature. Additionally, even specialised anger management programmes tend to presume and require a certain level of verbal expressive communication. For example, a feature of some anger management programmes is that of screening out prospective clients on the basis that they experience verbal expression difficulties (Howells, Rogers and Wilcock 2000). Clearly, there is a pressing need for anger management tools that are responsive to the needs of people with varying levels of cognitive ability, but also to the needs of people who use a range of expressive communication approaches, including those that rely on non-verbal communication methods.

This anger management package is distinguished from other programmes in the area in that it is designed specifically for people with intellectual disability, including people with a range of cognitive abilities, as well as for people with complex communication needs. The package incorporates modified content and includes a heavy emphasis on pictographic materials, functioning both as visual learning aids for clients with cognitive limitations and as an augmentative communication medium for clients with complex communication needs. Additionally, the package was developed to reflect themes and content relevant to the lives of people with physical disabilities, and it incorporates adapted activities and techniques (e.g., modified relaxation) for this group.

The programme is based on the following principles:

- Group-based anger management programmes are an evidence-based form of intervention for anger control issues that are regularly and universally available to members of the community.

- People with a range of types of disabilities should be able to access the same kinds of interventions that are available to the general community, albeit in a modified, accessible format.

- Successful anger interventions need to take place on two levels, the first attempting to identify and address the source of the anger, and the second teaching participants coping skills so they can manage their anger effectively (McVilly 2002).

- Anger is a normal human emotion; hence, the objective of an anger management programme such as this one is not the elimination of anger. Rather, the objective is to encourage people to deal with anger in ways that are constructive and effective in achieving a desired outcome, and conversely, not in ways that are destructive or result in negative consequences for the person concerned.

- A group-based anger management programme is one vehicle for addressing anger control issues, but the decision with respect to the most appropriate form of intervention, or whether intervention is required at all, should be based on the consideration of individual circumstances.

The theoretical framework adopted in the package is consistent with Novaco's (1975) cognitive-behavioural conceptualisation of anger that since the time of its inception has been utilised by a number of researchers and practitioners (e.g., Benson 1992; King *et al.* 1999). The framework views anger as a reaction to a perceived threat in which the cognitive, behavioural and physiological responses are each targeted as areas for intervention.

Using the package

The programme comprises 12 sessions of two hours duration, each including a fifteen-minute break; however, some timing variations may occur from session to session as determined by the needs of the group. The 12 sessions are:

1. Introduction to Anger Management (1)
2. Introduction to Anger Management (2)
3. Learning about Feelings and Anger
4. Learning about Helpful and Unhelpful Ways of Dealing With Anger
5. Learning to Relax (1)
6. Learning to Relax (2)
7. Learning to Think Calmly (1)
8. Learning to Think Calmly (2)
9. Learning to Think Calmly (3)
10. Learning to Handle Problems
11. Learning to Speak Up for Ourselves
12. Putting it all Together

Each session is fully scripted and follows a standard format, beginning with a review of skills learned during the previous session, followed by an introduction and explanation of the major session topic, then addressing the key learning aims for that session. However, given the nature of this type of group, it is important to emphasise that while a script is provided, it may not always be possible to adhere rigidly to it. Each session is effectively a self-contained unit. It is vital that the sessions are delivered in the sequence in which they appear in the package because content from one session builds on that from previous sessions. It is also important that all sessions are presented. All materials (excluding audio-visual resources) are provided in the package (including facilitator's script, hand-outs and evaluation sheets). Note that overheads are also included in the package, but these will need to be copied onto transparencies.

As indicated, the hand-outs have a strong emphasis on pictographic symbols and these can be used as an expressive communication medium for people with complex communication needs. It is recommended that for individuals with complex communication needs, facilitators also utilise established communication systems (e.g., electronic communication aids) and other communication methods (e.g., gestures and signs). It is important to acknowledge that even with the use of pictographs, some individuals may still exhibit comprehension and expression difficulties. Individuals in this circumstance may require content modifications or more individualised support. Additionally, facilitators may need to provide an explanation about specific pictographs to aid understanding of these.

The sessions are developed in accordance with basic learning principles. Active learning is emphasised in that participants are actively encouraged to be involved in sessions rather than being passive observers. Role-play is used with the aim of giving participants opportunities to practise behaviours in hypothetical situations that can then be generalised to real-life situations. Repetition is also used to reinforce the learning of concepts and skills.

Clearly, the facilitator will have a key role in relation to the delivery of the package material, the timing of sessions, and any adjustments to the content. At a more general level, the facilitator will need to have effective group leadership skills and a strong grounding in group dynamics. The facilitator will also need to be responsive to the needs of individuals with a range of levels of cognitive ability and/or complex communication needs. The package requires that the facilitator has existing knowledge of cognitive behaviour techniques.

In addition to these general suggestions, based on the writers' experiences in delivering the package, the following recommendations are offered to facilitators:

1. Include six to eight participants in each group.

2. Seat participants in an inclusive way, such as in a horseshoe ar.rangement.

3. Use an overhead projector to display overheads. Above and beyond the use of hand-outs, the use of overheads has been found to further aid the comprehension and retention of information for some participants.

4. Have access to a whiteboard, and use this where needed.

5. Participants may need an opportunity to practise role-plays prior to their demonstration in front of the group.

6. Consider offering participants an individual session at the completion of the formal program to review progress and identify future objectives.

7. Use a folder or equivalent to store hand-outs, because having too many loose hand-outs may be distracting for some participants.

8. Be aware that from time to time, participants may volunteer information that is of an overly personal nature, or not appropriate for group discussion. In such instances, the facilitator will need to manage these issues sensitively and redirect the topic of discussion.

Session 1

Introduction to Anger Management (1)

Aims of this session

1. Introduce participants to each other.
2. Have participants get to know each other a little better.
3. Present the rules of group work.
4. Introduce the concept of anger and anger management.

Materials required

- 'Getting to know each other' sheets.
- 'Group rules' sheets.
- Overhead: Anger can become a problem when...
- Overhead: Steps for learning to manage anger.

Session plan

Introduce participants to each other

- Introduce facilitator.

- Welcome group participants.

- Present a brief overview of the purpose of the group – to further develop our anger management skills.

- Have each member and their support person introduce themselves.

- Discuss 'housekeeping' issues (e.g., time of group, location of group, location of amenities).

Have participants get to know each other a little better

Emphasise that before beginning to discuss anger management, it is important that we get to know each other a little better.

ACTIVITY 1.1

Ask participants to form groups of two (preferably with someone they are unfamiliar with). Participants interview each other using the 'Getting to know each other' sheets. At the completion of the interviews, ask participants to report back their interview information.

For example, Brian has got to know Mary.
    'Brian, who did you get to know?'
    'Where does Mary live?'

Getting to know each other (1)

 **What is your name?**

_____

 **Who did you get to know?**

_____

 **Where does this person live?**

_____

Getting to know each other (2)

What does this person do during the week?

_____

What does this person like to do in their free time?

_____

What does this person want to get out of this group?

_____

> **Review 1.1**
>
> So far today we have:
>
> - got to know each other a little better. This is to help us feel more comfortable with each other.

Present rules of group work

Now we discuss some of the rules of group work. Emphasise that for groups to run effectively and smoothly, we need some basic rules. These rules will help each person get the most out of the programme.

ACTIVITY 1.2

Ask if any participants have been involved in group work before, their experiences of this, and what things have helped these groups run well. Present participants with the 'Group rules' sheets and discuss each of these points. Emphasise that it is important that:

- we are on time

- we attend all sessions

- we listen to each other

- we have only one person talking at a time

- we participate as much as we feel comfortable with

- we respect confidentiality

- we respect each other's ideas

- we try to stay calm – we don't lose our cool

- we have set breaks.

✓

Group rules (1)

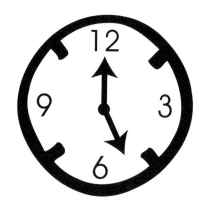 We are on time

 We attend all sessions

 We listen to each other

Group rules (2)

 We have only one person talking at a time

 We participate as much as we feel comfortable with

 We respect confidentiality

We respect each other's ideas

We try to stay calm – we don't lose our cool

We have set breaks

Review 1.2

So far today we have:

- got to know each other a little better
- talked about some of the rules of working in a group. This is to help the group run well.

Introduce the concepts of anger and anger management

Now we will begin to discuss anger and anger management. Ask participants what they think is meant by *anger*. Emphasise that anger is a normal human feeling that we all experience from time to time. Anger may occur when we feel threatened by something or someone. Different things can threaten each of us. The threat may be something that is quite real, such as when someone is about to hurt us. However, the threat may not be something physical; it may be something that affects us personally, such as when someone criticises us or hurts our feelings.

Anger can become a problem when...

- it happens a lot
- it happens too strongly
- it happens for too long
- we harm ourselves, others or property
- it affects our lives

Show the overhead 'Anger can become a problem when…' Emphasise that although anger is a normal feeling, anger can become a problem when:

- we experience anger a lot more often than other people do

- we experience very strong feelings of anger

- we experience anger for much longer than other people do

- it leads to harm to ourselves or others, or damage to property

- it leads to problems at work, in personal relationships and in the overall quality of life.

Ask participants about their personal experiences in these areas. For example, ask participants, 'How often do you get angry?', or 'How long do you stay angry?'

Steps for learning to manage anger

- Understanding the situation
- Understanding our reactions
- Learning and practising new ways
- Finding supports

123

Show the overhead 'Steps for learning to manage anger'. Emphasise that learning to manage our anger involves a number of steps, including:

- understanding the situations that lead us to feel angry

- understanding the ways we deal with our anger now

- learning and practising ways of handling our anger more effectively

- looking at the sorts of supports we need to achieve more effective ways of dealing with anger.

Inform participants that they will move through these steps as part of this programme.

Summary of Session 1

Today we have:

- got to know each other a little better

- talked about some of the rules of working in a group

- talked about anger and anger management.

Introduction to Anger Management (2)

Aims of this session

1. Briefly review summary points from the previous session.
2. Further explore the concepts of anger and anger management.
3. Conduct a brief self-assessment of anger.
4. Present an overview of the material to be covered in the sessions.

Materials required

- 'Managing anger well' sheet.
- 'Managing anger poorly' sheet.
- 'Anger' cards.
- 'Brief self-assessment of anger' sheets.
- 'Anger management programme overview' sheet.

Session plan

Briefly review summary points from the previous session

Present the summary points from the previous session.

Further explore the concepts of anger and anger management

ACTIVITY 2.1

Have participants form two groups. One group identifies the consequences for people when they manage anger well. The other group identifies the consequences for people when they manage their anger poorly. Responses are recorded on the 'Managing anger' sheets. These sheets include three areas where anger can have a consequence: feelings, relationships and capacity to handle difficulties. Participants should then share their responses with the wider group.

Emphasise that people who manage their anger well tend to:

- feel better about themselves. Their thoughts, feelings and bodies stay in control.

- be better at getting along with others, such as friends, family and staff. Others enjoy their company and they have better relationships with them.

- be better at handling difficulties, such as disappointments or criticism or problems.

Managing anger well

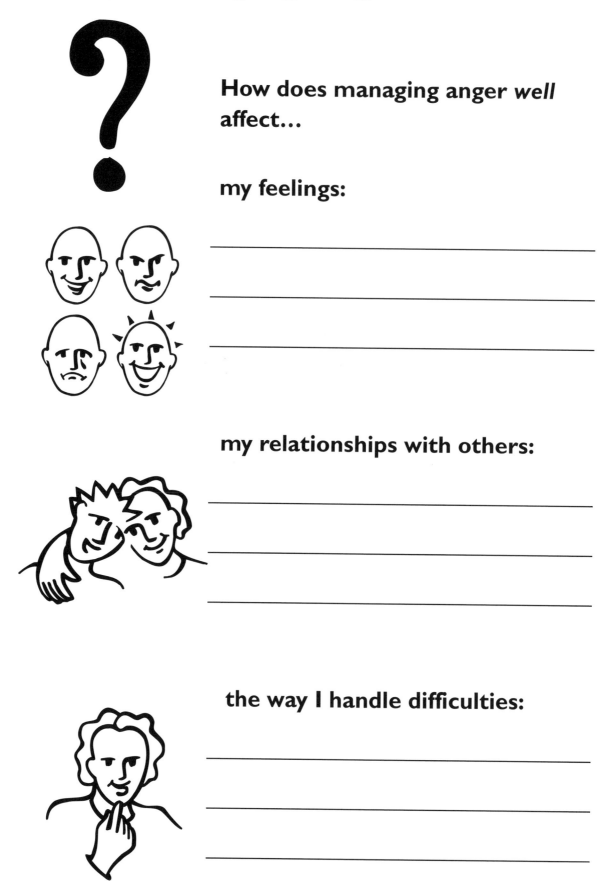

How does managing anger *well*
affect…

my feelings:

_____

_____

_____

my relationships with others:

_____

_____

_____

the way I handle difficulties:

_____

_____

_____

Managing anger poorly

How does managing anger _poorly_ affect...

my feelings:

_____

_____

_____

my relationships with others:

_____

_____

_____

the way I handle difficulties:

_____

_____

_____

ACTIVITY 2.2

Ask participants why it is that some people are good at handling their anger, while others have problems in handling their anger. Cut out the 'Anger' cards and have participants select a card that reflects one of these factors. You should then discuss this as a group. Factors include:

- having learnt 'bad habits'
- being tired
- personality
- lack of sleep
- lack of opportunities
- noise
- overcrowding
- lack of choice
- lack of support
- personal difficulties with others.

Anger cards

 Having learnt bad habits

 Being tired

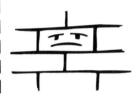 Personality

 Lack of sleep

 Lack of opportunities

 Noise

 Overcrowding

 Lack of choice

 Lack of support

 Personal difficulties with others

> **Review 2.1**
>
> So far today we have:
>
> - talked more about anger and anger management. We said that it's important to manage our anger well.

Conduct a brief self-assessment of anger

Let's look at our own anger, some of the things that contribute to our anger, and some of the ways we deal with anger.

ACTIVITY 2.3

For this activity, participants complete the 'Brief self-assessment of anger' sheets. Participants individually complete the sheet with assistance from their support person if required. Participants then present their responses to the group.

Brief self-assessment of anger (1)

I lose my temper quickly   ☐ Yes   ☐ No

Sometimes I fly off the handle   ☐ Yes   ☐ No

I get angry more than others   ☐ Yes   ☐ No

I have trouble controlling my temper   ☐ Yes   ☐ No

✓

Brief self-assessment of anger (2)

Sometimes I feel like 'exploding' ☐ Yes ☐ No

Some of my friends think I have a bad temper ☐ Yes ☐ No

I have difficulty thinking calmly ☐ Yes ☐ No

When I am angry I feel like lashing out ☐ Yes ☐ No

Review 2.2

So far today we have:

- talked about anger and anger management
- learnt a bit more about our own anger.

Present an overview of material to be covered in the sessions

Emphasise that we can learn better ways of dealing with our anger. Over the next few sessions, we will learn more about anger and how to handle our anger in a better way. Provide participants with the 'Anger management programme overview' sheet. Emphasise that the sessions we will cover are:

- learning about feelings and anger
- learning about helpful and unhelpful ways of dealing with anger
- learning to relax
- learning more ways to relax
- learning to think calmly
- learning more ways to think calmly
- learning even more ways to think calmly
- learning to speak up for ourselves
- learning to handle problems
- putting it all together.

Anger management programme overview

Session Number	Session	Date
1	Introduction to Anger Management (1)	
2	Introduction to Anger Management (2)	
3	Learning About Feelings and Anger	
4	Learning About Helpful and Unhelpful Ways of Dealing with Anger	
5	Learning to Relax (1)	
6	Learning to Relax (2)	
7	Learning to Think Camly (1)	
8	Learning to Think Camly (2)	
9	Learning to Think Camly (3)	
10	Learning to Handle Problems	
11	Learning to Speak Up for Ourselves	
12	Putting it all Together	

To help us learn about these areas, we will talk about them and use activities. We will also set goals that are important for participants to follow up on when they finish the sessions (with help from their support person if needed).

Summary of Session 2

Today we have:

- talked more about anger and anger management
- learnt a bit more about our own anger
- talked about what we are going to learn about in our sessions.

Session 3

Learning about Feelings and Anger

Aims of this session

1. Briefly review summary points from the previous session.

2. Explore a range of common feelings and their recognition.

3. Discuss what anger is and identify situations in which individuals feel angry.

4. Explore the physical, cognitive and behavioural changes experienced by individuals when they are angry.

Materials required

- 'Feelings' cards.
- Overhead: Facts about feelings.
- 'Feelings' prompt sheets.
- 'I feel angry when…' sheet.
- Overhead: Anger: Physical changes.
- 'Body' sheets.
- Stickers (to be provided by the facilitator).
- Overhead: Anger: Changes in thinking.
- Overhead: Anger: Changes in behaviour.
- 'Changes I experience when angry' sheet.

Session plan

Briefly review summary points from the previous session

Present summary points from the previous session.

Explore a range of common feelings and their recognition

Ask participants what they think is meant by *feelings*? Emphasise that feelings are the different emotions and moods we experience inside. Ask participants to identify some feelings they have had (e.g., happy, sad, excited, angry, frightened, proud, jealous).

ACTIVITY 3.1

Cut out the 'Feelings' cards. Participants select a card, then indicate a situation where they experienced that feeling. Ask other participants whether they have felt similarly. The 'Feelings' cards comprise the following feelings:

- happy
- sad
- scared
- proud
- worried
- angry
- excited
- surprised.

Feelings cards

Happy

Sad

Scared

Proud

Worried

Angry

Excited

Surprised

Show the overhead 'Facts about feelings'. Emphasise the following facts about feelings:

- We all experience feelings such as anger, happiness and sadness, at different times.

- It's OK to have these and other feelings.

- Sometimes our feelings can be the same as those of other people.

- Sometimes our feelings can be different from those of other people.

- Our feelings belong to us and we are responsible for them.

Facts about feelings

- We all experience feelings

- It's OK to experience feelings

- Our feelings can be the same as those of others

- Our feelings can be different from those of others

- Our feelings belong to us and we are responsible for them

ACTIVITY 3.2

Read out a situation to the group from the 'Feelings' prompt sheets. Each participant identifies the feeling/s they would probably have in that situation and shares them with the group. Emphasise that for any particular situation, our feelings can be the same as or different from those of other people. The situations are as follows:

- You are given a special job to do for the first time.

- You receive an award for a special achievement.

- You see a family member you have not seen for a while.

- Someone gives you a surprise present.

- Someone tells you to shut up.

- The taxi doesn't arrive on time.

- Someone says that you are very special to them.

- You lose your money.

- You are invited to go to a party.

- You hear a loud noise in the middle of the night.

- Someone says your new shirt is awful.

- Someone changes the TV channel while you are watching TV.

Feelings prompt sheet (1)

 You are given a special job to do for the first time

 You receive an award for a special achievement

 You see a family member you have not seen for a while

 Someone gives you a surprise present

Feelings prompt sheet (2)

 Someone tells you to shut up

 The taxi does not arrive on time

 Someone says that you are very special to them

 You lose your money

Feelings prompt sheet (3)

 You are invited to go to a party

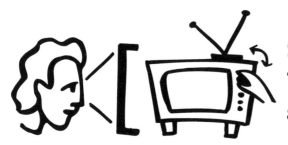 You hear a loud noise in the middle of the night

 Someone says your new shirt is awful

 Someone changes the TV channel while you are watching TV

Review 3.1

So far today we have:

- learnt about feelings. We said that we can experience a range of feelings and that our feelings can be the same as and also different to the feelings of other people.

Discuss what anger is and identify situations in which individuals feel angry

We said in the last session that anger is a normal human feeling that we all experience from time to time. Many different things can lead us to feel angry. The sorts of things that make us feel angry vary from person to person. For example, someone may feel angry when spoken to in a loud voice. But another person may *not* feel angry in the same situation. Let's explore the situations in which we each feel angry.

ACTIVITY 3.3

Ask participants to individually complete the 'I feel angry when…' sheet. Responses are then presented to the rest of the group. Emphasise that it is important to recognise the situations in which we feel angry. By doing so, we can be aware of our responses and make changes to the way we handle anger.

I feel angry when...

When do I feel angry?

_____

_____

_____

_____

_____

_____

_____

_____

_____

_____

Review 3.2

Up until now we have:

- learnt about feelings

- learnt about anger, and situations in which we may feel angry. It is important for us to be aware of these situations if we are to change the way we deal with anger.

Explore the physical, cognitive and behavioural changes experienced by individuals when they are angry

When we feel angry, we may experience changes in our body, our thoughts and our behaviour. We will now look at each of these types of changes.

Physical changes

Show the overhead 'Anger: Physical changes' and tell the participants that when we feel angry, our bodies react differently. Changes may include:

- pupils dilate (our eyes become wider)

- muscles tense up

- facial expression changes

- stomach aches

- heart rate increases

- fists clench

- teeth clench

- start to sweat or feel cold

- blush.

Anger – Physical changes

- Pupils dilate
- Muscles tense up
- Facial expression changes
- Stomach aches
- Heart rate increases
- Fists clench
- Teeth clench
- Get sweaty
- Feel cold
- Blush

ACTIVITY 3.4

Ask the participants to use the 'Body sheet' to indicate the part of their body most affected when they feel angry. Participants can use stickers (or some other form of marker) to show the affected body parts. Participants complete the activity individually then present their responses to the rest of the group.

Body sheet (F)

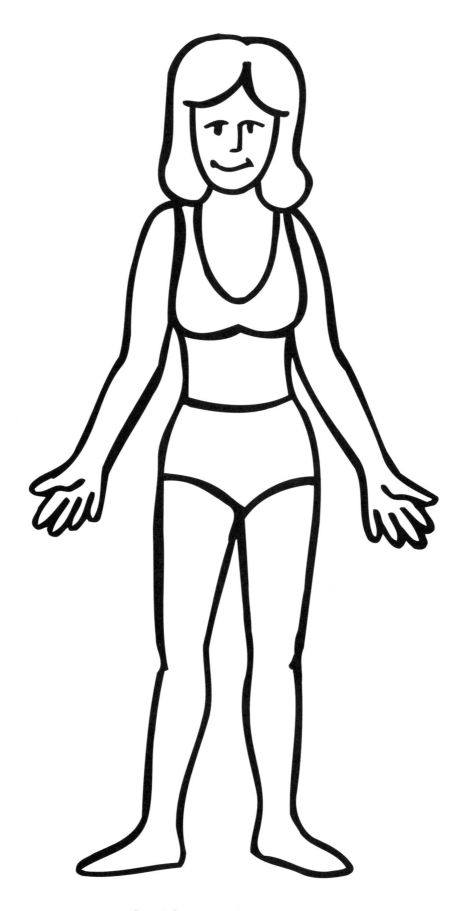

Body sheet (M)

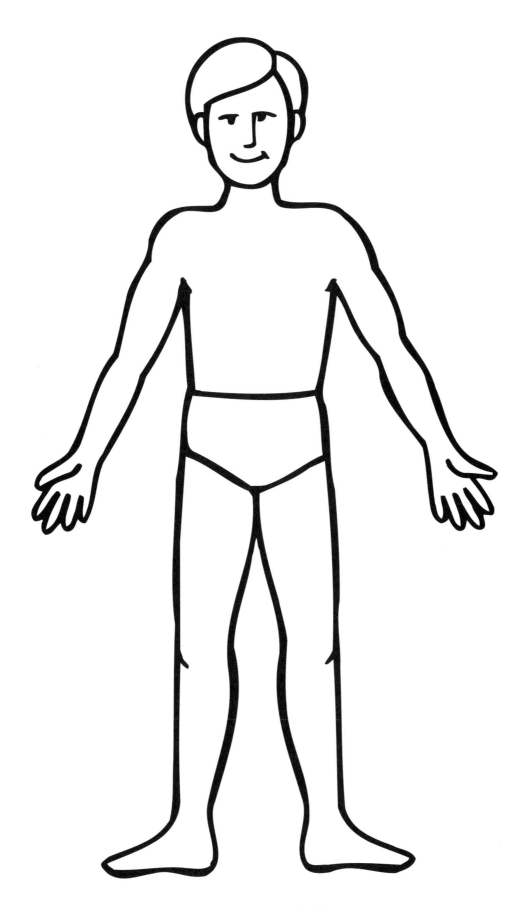

CHANGES IN THINKING

Show the overhead 'Anger: Changes in thinking', and tell participants that when we feel angry, our thinking can also change. Some of the thoughts we may have are:

- This is awful.

- I can't stand this.

- I hate this.

- I've had enough.

- I'm going to get him.

- I'm going to explode.

- I don't care.

Anger – Changes in thinking

- **This is awful**

- **I can't stand this**

- **I hate this**

- **I've had enough**

- **I'm going to get him**

- **I'm going to explode**

- **I don't care**

ACTIVITY 3.5

As a brainstorming exercise, ask participants to identify some of the thoughts they have when they are angry.

CHANGES IN BEHAVIOUR

Show the overhead: 'Anger: Changes in behaviour', and tell participants that when we feel angry, the ways we behave can also change. Some of the things we may do are:

- walk away
- withdraw
- hit others
- yell
- shout
- swear
- mope around
- throw things.

As a brainstorming exercise, ask participants to identify some of the ways their behaviour changes when they are angry.

Anger – Changes in behaviour

- Walk away
- Withdraw
- Hit others
- Yell
- Shout
- Swear
- Mope around
- Throw things

ACTIVITY 3.6

Ask participants to complete the 'Changes I experience when angry' sheet. Participants identify an example of a change they experience in their body, thinking and behaviour associated with anger. Participants present their responses to the group. Emphasise that when we are angry, we may experience a range of changes in ourselves.

Changes I experience when angry

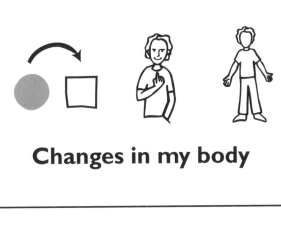

Changes in my body

_____

_____

_____

Changes in my thoughts

_____

_____

_____

Changes in my behaviour (things I do)

_____

_____

_____

Summary of Session 3

Today we have:

- learnt about feelings

- learnt about anger, and situations in which we may feel angry

- talked about some of the changes we experience when we are angry. We can experience changes in our bodies, our thoughts and our behaviour.

Learning about Helpful and Unhelpful Ways of Dealing with Anger

Aims of this session

1. Briefly review summary points from the previous session.
2. Discuss helpful and unhelpful ways of dealing with anger.

Materials required

- Whiteboard (optional).
- Overhead: Helpful versus unhelpful ways of dealing with anger.
- Overhead: People who use helpful ways.
- Overhead: People who use unhelpful ways.
- 'Helpful/unhelpful ways of dealing with anger' cards and boxes.
- 'My ways of dealing with anger' sheet.

Session plan

Briefly review summary points from the previous session

Present summary points from the previous session.

Discuss helpful and unhelpful ways of dealing with anger

Show the overhead 'Helpful versus unhelpful ways of dealing with anger' and tell the participants that while anger is a normal feeling, it's *what we do* when we feel angry that's important. When it comes to dealing with anger, there are two paths we can take. We can choose to deal with anger in helpful ways, or we can choose to deal with anger in unhelpful ways.

When we use helpful ways of dealing with anger we recognise and express our anger in appropriate and constructive ways. This means we still deal with our anger, but in a way that doesn't hurt others or ourselves and doesn't make things worse for us.

When we use unhelpful ways of dealing with anger we express our anger in inappropriate and destructive ways. This means we deal with our anger in ways that can hurt others or ourselves and may make things worse for us.

Helpful versus unhelpful ways of dealing with anger

When we deal with anger in a way that:

- doesn't hurt others or ourselves

- doesn't make things worse for us

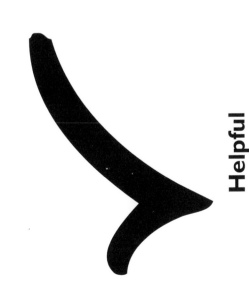

Helpful

When we deal with anger in a way that:

- can hurt ourselves or others

- makes things worse for ourselves

Unhelpful

Show the overhead 'People who use helpful ways', and tell participants that it's important we try to deal with our anger in helpful ways. Emphasise that people who deal with anger using helpful ways are more likely to:

- feel better about themselves because they stay in control of their feelings and behaviour

- have their needs met in a way that is respectful to others

- come out of a threatening situation with less negative effects on them personally

- gain respect from others because they deal with their anger well

- get along better with others, such as friends, family and staff

- handle negative experiences better, such as disappointments, criticism or problems.

People who use helpful ways

- stay in control
- can get what they want
- experience fewer negative consequences
- gain respect
- get along with others
- can handle difficulties

ACTIVITY 4.1

Let's look at some helpful ways of dealing with anger.

Ask participants to identify and list some helpful ways of dealing with anger. This can be done as a group 'brainstorming' activity with responses written on a whiteboard (optional). Emphasise that some helpful ways of dealing with anger include:

- being aware of what makes us angry

- communicating our feelings clearly and openly

- taking some time out when things get difficult

- learning ways to relax

- saying things to ourselves that help us stay calm

- trying to solve the problem.

Show the overhead 'People who use unhelpful ways' and tell participants that it's important we try to avoid using unhelpful ways of dealing with anger. Emphasise that people who deal with anger using unhelpful ways are more likely to:

- lose control of their feelings and behaviour

- get their feelings across, but in a way that is not respectful to others

- experience negative consequences as a result of their behaviour

- not be respected by others because they deal with their anger poorly

- have difficulties getting along with others

- handle negative experiences poorly.

People who use unhelpful ways

- lose control
- get feelings across but without respecting others
- experience negative consequences
- lose the respect of others
- don't get along with others
- don't handle difficulties well

ACTIVITY 4.2

Let's look at some unhelpful ways of dealing with anger.

Now ask participants to identify and list some unhelpful ways of dealing with anger. Responses can be written in a separate section on the whiteboard (optional). Emphasise that some unhelpful ways of dealing with anger include:

- ignoring the things that make us angry
- keeping feelings 'bottled up'
- blaming others
- taking your anger out on others
- thinking negatively
- letting the problem continue
- becoming violent towards others, yourself or property.

ACTIVITY 4.3

Cut out the 'Helpful/unhelpful ways of dealing with anger' cards. Ask each participant to select a card and judge whether the response is helpful or unhelpful. Participants use the 'Helpful ways' and 'Unhelpful ways' boxes to sort their responses (facilitators will need to construct the boxes for this activity, or alternatively, provide pre-constructed boxes). The responses appearing on the cards are summarised below:

- finding someone to talk with
- getting help to solve the problem
- going to a quiet room
- hitting someone
- keeping your feelings bottled up
- kicking the wall
- putting on some relaxing music
- screaming and crying
- telling yourself, 'I can't cope with this.'
- telling yourself, 'Calm down.'
- walking away
- yelling at others.

Helpful/unhelpful ways of dealing with anger cards (1)

Finding someone to talk with

Getting help to solve the problem

Going to a quiet room

Hitting someone

Keeping your feelings bottled up

Kicking the wall

Helpful/unhelpful ways of dealing with anger cards (2)

Putting on some relaxing music

Screaming and crying

I can't do this..

Telling yourself, 'I can't cope with this'.

Calm down

Telling youself to 'calm down'.

Walking away

Yelling at others

Helpful ways box

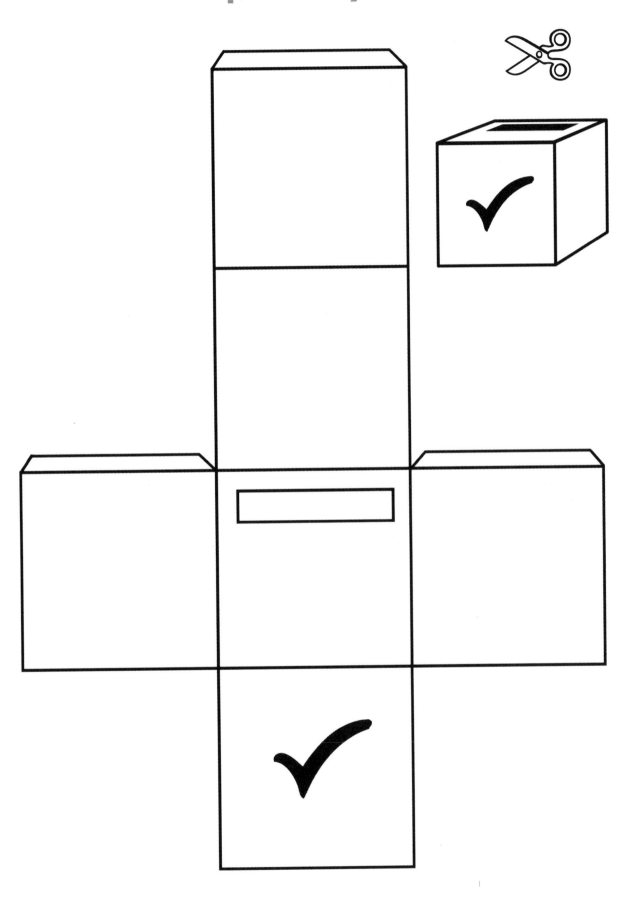

Unhelpful ways box

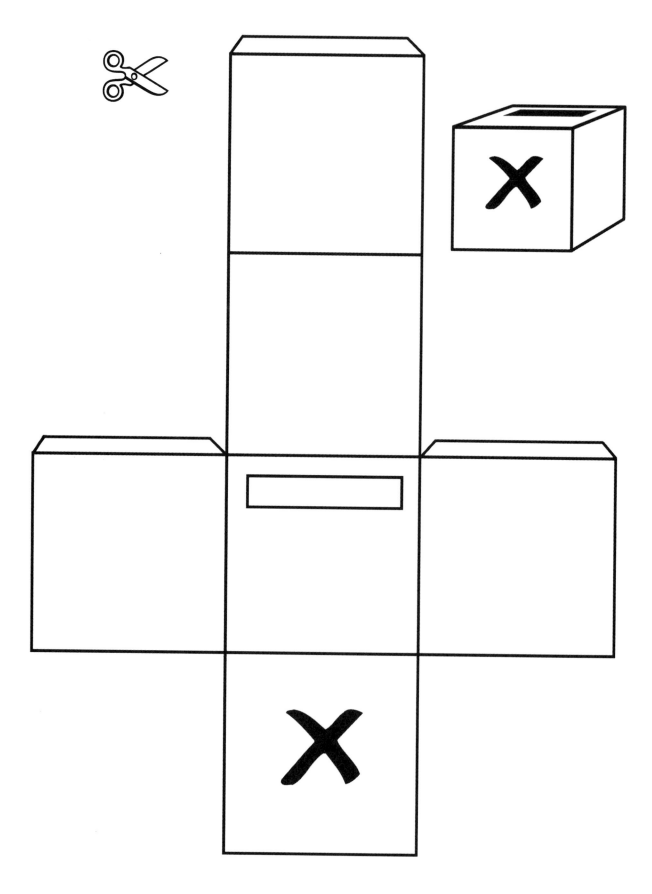

ACTIVITY 4.4

Ask participants to complete the 'My ways of dealing with anger' sheet, indicating unhelpful and helpful method/s they each use to deal with anger. Emphasise that it is important we avoid unhelpful ways and focus on helpful ways when dealing with anger-provoking situations. Emphasise that we will learn more about helpful ways as we progress through the course.

✓

My ways of dealing with anger

Unhelpful ways...

_____

_____

_____

Helpful ways...

_____

_____

_____

Summary of Session 4

Today we have:

- discussed some of the different ways we react when angry
- discussed helpful and unhelpful ways of dealing with anger. We saw the differences between these two ways of dealing with anger and agreed it is important for us to deal with anger in helpful ways.

Session 5

Learning to Relax (1)

Aims of this session

1. Briefly review summary points from the previous session.
2. Discuss what relaxation is, and how it can assist us in dealing with anger.
3. Explore a range of relaxation techniques.

Materials required

- Overhead: Relaxation can help.
- Overhead: How can relaxation help you deal with anger?
- Overhead: Other benefits of relaxation.
- Overhead: When can relaxation be used?
- Overhead: Relaxation techniques.
- 'Deep breathing' tip sheet.
- 'Talking calmly to ourselves' tip sheet.
- 'Picture a calm scene' tip sheet.
- 'Count to 10' tip sheet.

Session plan

Briefly review summary points from the previous session

Present summary points from the previous session.

Discuss what relaxation is, and how it can assist us in dealing with anger

Emphasise to the participants that when we spoke about ways of dealing with anger, we said one of the helpful ways of dealing with anger is to learn to use relaxation. We will be learning about relaxation over the next two sessions.

Ask participants what they think is meant by *relaxation*. Emphasise that relaxation is a technique we can use to reduce stress. Relaxation is more than just engaging in a pleasurable activity, such as watching TV or listening to the radio. Rather, it is a focused attempt to relax the mind and body.

Show the overhead 'Relaxation can help', and tell participants that relaxation can help:

- calm the mind
- calm the body
- reduce tension
- increase calmness and control.

Relaxation can help

- calm the mind

- calm the body

- reduce tension

- increase calmness

- increase control

Show the overhead 'How can relaxation help you deal with anger?', and tell participants that relaxation can assist us to deal better with our feelings of anger. This is because:

- taking time out might give you a new view of the situation

- it can avoid things getting worse

- when you are relaxing, it takes you away from angry feelings.

How can relaxation help you deal with anger?

- Gives you time out

- Avoids things getting worse

- Takes you away from angry feelings

Show the overhead 'Other benefits of relaxation', and tell participants that relaxation can help us with our anger but it can also help us in other areas of our lives. Relaxation can help us to:

- be less irritable

- think better and enjoy improved concentration

- feel calmer, happier and more energetic

- enjoy more restful sleep

- increase our feeling of control

- regain control

- focus on ourselves

- improve body functions, such as decreasing heart rate, blood pressure, breathing rate and muscle tension.

Other benefits of relaxation

- **Be less irritable**

- **Think better**

- **Feel calmer**

- **Sleep better**

- **Feel in control**

- **Regain control**

- **Focus on ourselves**

- **Improve body functions**

Show the overhead 'When can relaxation be used?', and tell participants that relaxation can be used at different times. We can use relaxation to:

- prepare us for a difficult situation

- get us through a difficult situation

- help us wind down after a difficult situation is over.

When can relaxation be used?

- **Before a difficult situation**

- **During a difficult situation**

- **After a difficult situation**

Review 5.1

So far today we have:

- discussed what relaxation is and how it can help us deal with anger better.

Explore a range of relaxation techniques

Show the overhead 'Relaxation techniques', and tell participants that there are many ways we can relax. Today we will learn about some of these ways. Because each of us is different, each of us may find one of the methods more helpful than the others. The different methods we will learn about and try are:

- deep breathing
- talking calmly to ourselves
- picturing a calm scene
- counting to ten
- muscle relaxation.

Relaxation techniques

- **Deep breathing**

- **Talking calmly to ourselves**

- **Picturing a calm scene**

- **Counting to 10**

- **Muscle relaxation**

ACTIVITY 5.1

Ask participants to complete a deep breathing exercise. Emphasise that by becoming more aware of your own breathing and taking deep breaths, you can reduce tension. Have participants perform 'breath counting', encouraging them to:

1. Sit in a comfortable position.

2. Breathe in deeply, pause, then breathe out.

3. While breathing out, count 'One', then continue to count each outward breath by saying, 'Two... Three...'.

4. Continue to count outward breaths in sets of four for five minutes.

5. Notice their breathing gradually slowing throughout the exercise, their body relaxing, and their mind calming.

At the completion of the exercise, ask participants to feed back their experiences of this deep breathing exercise. Ask participants:

- how easy or hard it was to focus on the instructions

- whether or not they felt they achieved an overall state of relaxation.

Provide participants with the 'Deep breathing' tip sheet, and go over this information with them.

Deep breathing tip sheet

 **Sit in a comfortable position**

 **Breathe in deeply, then breathe out and keep doing this**

 **Count each breath 1...2...3...**

 **Continue for 5 minutes**

 **Notice your mind and body relaxing**

ACTIVITY 5.2

Ask participants to complete a calm self-talk exercise. Emphasise that by saying calm things to ourselves, we can reduce our tension and feel more positive about ourselves. Encourage participants to:

1. Close their eyes, if possible, and begin taking slow deep breaths.

2. Listen to a number of calm statements that are said by the facilitator:

   - I can cope with stress.

   - I can work out my problems.

   - I can handle it.

   - I can stay in control.

   - I can focus on my strengths.

   - I can have a bad day sometimes.

   - I can improve myself.

At the completion of the exercise, ask participants to talk about their experiences of the calm self-talk exercise. Ask participants:

- how easy or hard it was to focus on the instructions

- whether or not they felt they achieved an overall state of relaxation.

Provide participants with the 'Talking calmly to ourselves' tip sheet, and go over this information with them.

Talking calmly to ourselves tip sheet

 Close your eyes if possible

 Take slow deep breaths

 Think calm thoughts

I can cope with stress

I can work out my problems

I can handle it

I can stay in control

I can focus on my strengths

I can improve myself

ACTIVITY 5.3

Ask participants to complete a simple visualisation exercise. Emphasise that we will use our imagination to picture ourselves in a calm scene. This can help us feel more safe and relaxed. Encourage participants to:

1. Close their eyes, if possible, and begin taking slow deep breaths.

2. Listen to the words of the facilitator and try to picture themselves in the following scene.

    Picture yourself at the beach. The rays of the sun are soft and warm. You hear the sounds of the seagulls and the waves gently rolling. The waves roll in and out, in and out. Each wave makes you feel more and more relaxed. You can see the sand, and the waves and the blue sky. You can feel the cool salt air. You take deep breaths of the air and with each breath, you feel more and more relaxed. You feel safe and calm.

At the completion of the exercise, ask participants to discuss their experiences of this exercise. Ask them:

- how easy or hard it was to focus on the instructions

- whether or not they felt they achieved an overall state of relaxation.

Provide participants with the 'Picture a calm scene' tip sheet, and go over this information with them.

Picture a calm scene tip sheet

 **Close your eyes if possible**

 **Take slow deep breaths**

 **Use your imagination to picture yourself in a calm scene**

Picture yourself at the beach. The rays of the sun are soft and warm. You hear the sounds of the seagulls and the waves gently rolling. The waves roll in and out, in and out. Each wave makes you feel more and more relaxed. You can see the sand, and the waves and the blue sky. You can feel the cool salt air. You take deep breaths of the air and with each breath, you feel more and more relaxed. You feel safe and calm.

ACTIVITY 5.4

Ask participants to complete a simple counting exercise. Emphasise that through counting from 1 to 10, we can slowly help ourselves wind down and feel more relaxed. Encourage participants to:

1. Close their eyes, if possible, and begin taking slow deep breaths.

2. Listen to the facilitator as they count from 1 to 10 (alternatively, have a participant lead the count). The counting becomes progressively slower.

3. Throughout the exercise, ask participants to notice their body relaxing and their mind calming.

At the completion of the exercise, ask participants to discuss their experiences of this specific relaxation technique. Ask participants:

- how easy or hard it was to focus on the instructions

- whether or not they felt they achieved an overall state of relaxation.

Provide participants with the 'Count to 10' tip sheet, and go over this information with them.

✓

Count to 10 tip sheet

 **Close your eyes if possible**

 **Take slow deep breaths**

 **Count from 1 to 10**

1   2   3   4   5   6   7   8   9   10

Summary of Session 5

Today we have:

- discussed what relaxation is and how it can help us deal with anger better
- looked at some different ways of relaxing.

Session 6

Learning to Relax (2)

Aims of this session

1. Briefly review summary points from the previous session.

2. Explore a specific relaxation technique: muscle relaxation.

Materials required

- Overhead: Relaxation techniques, from the previous session (p.86).

- Relaxation for People with Disabilities CD (Easy Relaxation CD, Scope (Vic.) Ltd, distributed by Scope (Vic.) Ltd, 177 Glenroy Road, Glenroy, 3046, Australia, e-mail: contact@scopevic.org.au, order online at www.scopevic.org.au/info_publications.html) (to be provided by facilitator).

- 'Other tips for relaxing' sheets.

Session plan

Briefly review summary points from the previous session

Present summary points from the previous session.

Have participants review and practise each of the four relaxation methods covered in the last session, namely:

- deep breathing

- talking calmly to ourselves

- picturing a calm scene

- counting to 10.

Explore a specific relaxation technique: muscle relaxation

Emphasise to participants that in the last session we tried a number of exercises to help us feel less tense and more relaxed. Today, we will try one more technique, called muscle relaxation.

When we feel tense, angry or upset, certain muscles in our body become tight. We can feel less tense if we learn to relax these muscles. This is because relaxing your muscles helps your mind to relax. When your body and mind are relaxed, you are able to deal better with difficult situations. In this exercise we will relax some muscle groups in the body, one at a time. While we relax our muscles, we will also breathe slowly and deeply and think good thoughts.

Like all the other relaxation techniques we have learnt about, practice is very important. It is like learning any other skill, the more you practise, the better you get at it.

ACTIVITY 6.1

Participants listen to the Relaxation for People with Disabilities CD. This CD incorporates muscle relaxation techniques, as well as deep breathing and positive self-talk. The relaxation exercise takes 25 to 30 minutes. At the completion of the exercise, participants are asked to feed back their experiences of relaxation. Ask participants:

- which muscle groups were easier to relax

- which muscle groups were more difficult to relax

- how easy or hard was it to focus on the instructions

- whether or not they felt they achieved an overall state of relaxation.

Show the overhead 'Relaxation techniques' from the previous session (p.86), and say to participants that over the last two sessions, we have learnt some different ways of relaxing. To summarise the techniques we have talked about, we have learnt about:

- deep breathing

- talking calmly to ourselves

- picturing a calm scene

- counting to ten

- muscle relaxation.

Because we are all different, each of us may prefer a different relaxation technique. Ask participants to identify which techniques they felt worked best for them.

Emphasise that in addition to using some of the relaxation exercises we have just done, there are other things we can do to help ourselves feel more relaxed. Ask participants what some of the other things we can do to help ourselves feel more relaxed are.

ACTIVITY 6.2

Hand out the 'Other tips for relaxing' sheets. Emphasise that there are many other things we can do to help ourselves feel more relaxed:

- Develop new interests, hobbies and recreational activities.

- Do what you enjoy, such as watch a movie or talk with a friend.

- Relax regularly in your favourite way.

- Work out what worries you and try to find a solution. Get help if you need to.

- Get proper rest and nutrition.

- Treat yourself to something special every now and then.

- Have time-out from difficult situations or people.

- Keep a sense of humour.

Other tips for relaxing (1)

Develop new hobbies and interests

Do what you enjoy, like watching a movie or talking with a friend

Relax in your favourite way

Work out what worries you and find a solution

Other tips for relaxing (2)

Get proper rest and nutrition

Treat yourself to something special now and then

Have time out from difficult situations or people

Keep a sense of humour

Summary of Session 6

Today we have:

- practised a number of relaxation methods covered in the last session
- practised another type of relaxation (muscle relaxation), and looked at general strategies to help us relax.

Learning to Think Calmly (1)

Aims of this session

1. Briefly review summary points from the previous session.

2. Highlight the difference between calm thoughts and angry thoughts.

3. Discuss how angry thoughts impact on our feelings and behaviour.

Materials required

- 'Calm thoughts/angry thoughts' checklist.

- Overhead: Anger meter.

- 'Personal anger meter'.

Session plan

Briefly review summary points from the previous session

Present summary points from the previous session.

Highlight the difference between calm thoughts and angry thoughts

Emphasise to the participants that inside our heads, we all say things to ourselves. Sometimes we say things to ourselves that are cool and calm. When we have cool and calm thoughts, we are more likely to stay in control. But, sometimes, we say things to ourselves that are wild and angry. When we have angry and wild thoughts, we are more likely to get out of control. Let's look at the difference between calm thoughts and angry thoughts.

ACTIVITY 7.1

Ask participants to complete the 'Calm thoughts/angry thoughts' checklist. Ask them to indicate whether each statement reflects a calm thought or an angry thought. Responses are then discussed with the group.

Calm thoughts/angry thoughts checklist

	Calm	Angry
I can't handle this	☐	☐
Relax	☐	☐
Calm down	☐	☐
He always hurts me	☐	☐
I hate this	☐	☐
Stay in control	☐	☐
Think before you say something	☐	☐
I am losing control	☐	☐
Be careful	☐	☐
You can cope with this	☐	☐
Don't panic	☐	☐
I'll explode	☐	☐
I can't take this any longer	☐	☐
You can do it	☐	☐
I'm going to get him	☐	☐
Stop, think and plan	☐	☐
Get back at her	☐	☐
You are doing well	☐	☐
I blew it again	☐	☐
Take it easy	☐	☐

> **Review 7.1**
>
> So far today we have:
>
> - seen the difference between calm and angry thoughts. This is to help us be more aware of how we think.

Discuss how angry thoughts impact on our feelings and behaviour

Ask participants how we feel and how we behave when we think calm thoughts. Emphasise that calm thoughts help us stay in control of our feelings and our behaviour. Ask participants how we feel and how we behave when we think angry thoughts. Emphasise that angry thoughts work against us. They can lead us to lose control of our feelings and our behaviour.

ACTIVITY 7.2

Ask one participant to role-play the same situation using two styles of thinking: angry thinking and calm thinking. The rest of the group are asked to observe and comment on the two types of thinking and how they impact on the person's feelings and behaviour. Facilitators should instruct the participants on how they should perform the role-play.

Angry thinking

- Set the scene: The participant comes to the kitchen in the morning wanting a cup of coffee. They discover that there is no coffee left. Ask the participant to tell the group what they are thinking (e.g., 'What are you thinking now?'). The participant shares their thoughts, which are, 'No one cares,' 'I hate living here,' 'It must be that awful person who has finished it off.'

- The participant role-plays: He/she starts yelling and throws the cup.

Calm thinking

- Set the scene: The participant comes to the kitchen in the morning wanting a cup of coffee. They discover that there is no coffee left. Ask the participant to tell the group what they are thinking (e.g., 'What are you thinking now?'). The participant shares their thoughts, which are, 'Take it easy,' 'It's not worth it,' 'I'll go to the next unit and ask for some coffee.'

- The participant role-plays: He/she says, 'Why throw the cup? I'll go to the next unit and get some coffee.'

Emphasise that our feelings and behaviour are affected by our thinking.

Let's look more closely at how our feelings and behaviour are affected by our thoughts. The calmer our thoughts are, the calmer we will behave. The angrier our thoughts are, the angrier we will feel and behave. Let's look at what our thoughts are at different stages of our anger.

ACTIVITY 7.3

Introduce the overhead 'Anger meter'. Emphasise that we will use the anger meter to identify our level of anger. When the barometer is low, we are in control of our feelings and behaviour. Our anger is usually at this level when our thoughts are cool and calm. When the barometer is high, we may lose control of our feelings and behaviour. Our anger is usually at this level when our thoughts are wild and angry. Use the following example:

> John is washing the dishes and feels like he is doing a good job. The supervisor approaches John and says, 'That's terrible. Those dishes are still dirty. You'll have to do them again.'

Ask participants to indicate John's level of anger (on the anger meter) when he is thinking the following thoughts:

- 'That doesn't bother me. I think I've done a pretty good job.'

- 'That annoys me, but I'm not going to get too angry about it.'

- 'I'm really angry.'

- 'I can't stand him. I'm furious.'

Now have participants identify their own thoughts at different stages of their anger on their 'Personal anger meter'. Ask participants to think of a recent situation when they felt angry. Ask participants to identify their thoughts when they were calm (just before the incident), when they were starting to get angry, when they were angry and when they were furious. Emphasise that the more intense our thoughts are, the more intense our feelings and behaviours are. Emphasise also that it is important that we are aware of our thinking and catch ourselves early to avoid our thinking and our behaviour getting out of control.

Anger meter

My feelings

- Furious
- Angry
- Getting angry
- Calm

My thoughts

- I can't stand it – I'm furious
- I'm really angry
- That annoys me but I'm not going to get angry
- That doesn't bother me

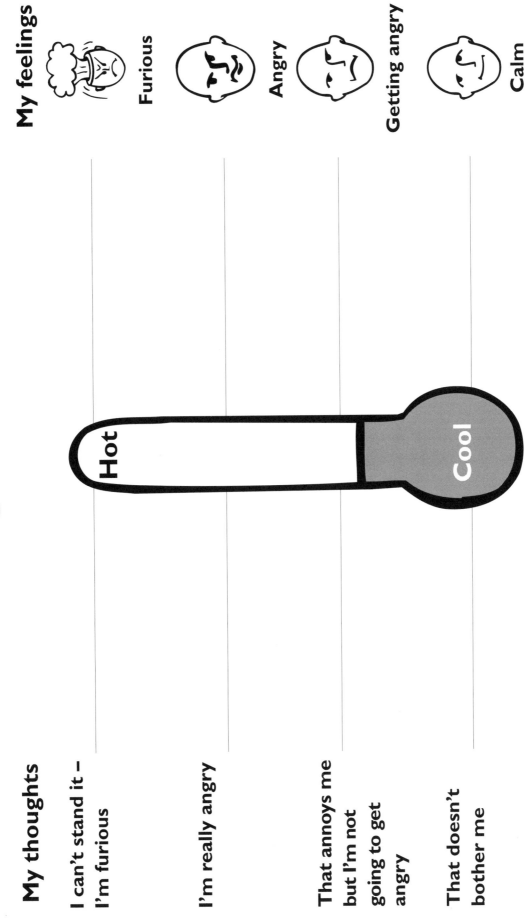

Hot

Cool

Personal anger meter

My thoughts

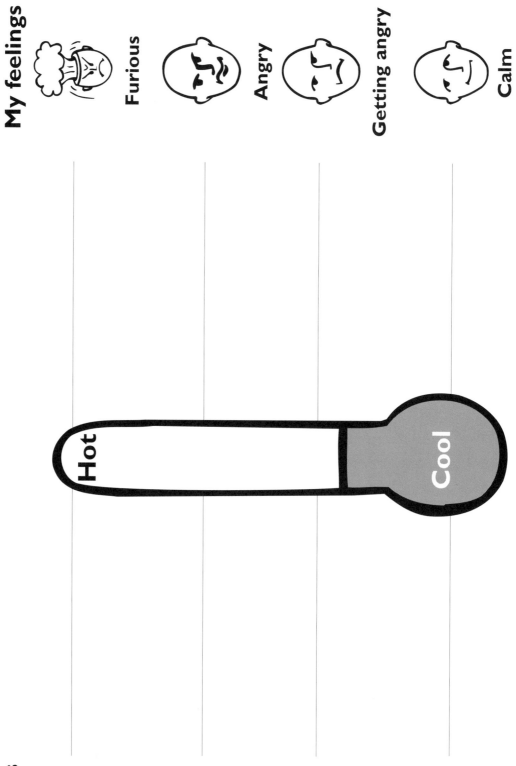

Hot

Cool

My feelings

Furious

Angry

Getting angry

Calm

Summary of Session 7

Today we have:

- seen the difference between calm and angry thoughts. This is to help us be more aware of how we think.

- seen that our thoughts can affect the way we feel and behave. When we think calm thoughts, we are more likely to stay in control. When we think angry thoughts, we are more likely to lose control.

Learning to Think Calmly (2)

Aims of this session

1. Briefly review summary points from the previous session.
2. Explore how self-calming statements can decrease anger.
3. Develop personal coping statements to deal with anger.

Materials required

- 'Thinking/feeling' sheet.
- 'A situation when I felt angry' sheet.
- Overhead: Self-calming statements can be used.
- 'Self-calming statements' sheets.
- 'Personal coping statements' sheet.

Session plan

Briefly review summary points from the previous session

Present summary points from the previous session.

Explore how self-calming statements can decrease anger

Remind participants that in the last session, we saw how our thoughts can affect the way we feel and behave. Let's look more closely at how our thoughts affect our feelings and our behaviour.

ACTIVITY 8.1

Use the 'Thinking/feeling sheet' to explain the concept of the relationship between our thoughts and responses. Emphasise that it is our interpretation of the situation that largely determines our feelings and our behaviours. If we interpret events in a negative way, we are likely to experience/show negative feelings and behaviours. If we interpret events in a calm way, we are likely to experience/show calm feelings and behaviours. Give the following examples:

Situation: You need to go to work by bus. The bus is late.

Thought: 'This is terrible – this bus is always late. I'll be late for work. My supervisor will be so upset with me!'

Feelings: Anger.

Behaviour: Pacing up and down, yelling.

Thought: 'This is not great. I might be late for work. I'll call and let them know. My supervisor will understand.'

Feelings: Annoyed but able to cope.

Behaviour: Calm and in control.

Now the facilitator asks the participants to complete the 'A situation when I felt angry' sheet. Ask participants to think about a recent situation where they have felt angry. Ask participants to write down what the situation was, what their thoughts were, how they felt and how they behaved. Participants share their responses with the group.

Thinking/feeling sheet

This is AWFUL

It's not great but I can get through this

You feel angry

You feel annoyed but able to cope

You start to yell

You stay calm and in control

A situation when I felt angry

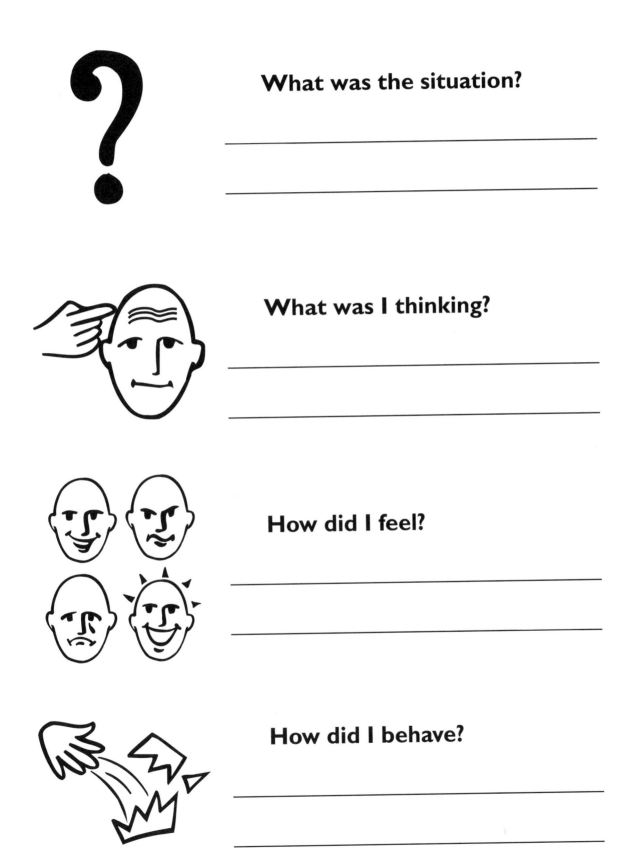

What was the situation?

_____

_____

What was I thinking?

_____

_____

How did I feel?

_____

_____

How did I behave?

_____

_____

Show the overhead 'Self-calming statements can be used', and tell participants that now that we have seen how our thoughts can impact on our feelings and behaviour, we can look more closely at self-calming statements. Self-calming statements are cool and level-headed things we can say to ourselves to help us stay in control. These are things like, 'I will get through this,' 'I can cope,' and 'It's over now. I made it through.'

Self-calming statements can be used:

- before going into a situation where we know we might feel angry

- during a situation where we are feeling angry

- after a situation where we have felt angry.

Self-calming statements can be used

- before a difficult situation

- during a difficult situation

- after a difficult situation

ACTIVITY 8.2

Ask participants to identify self-calming statements they can use before, during and after an anger-provoking event. Do this as a group brainstorming exercise. Then hand out the 'Self-calming statements' sheets. Emphasise that on the sheets are written a number of self-calming statements that can be used before, during and after an anger-provoking event. These are:

Before:

- It will only last for a short while.
- I can ask for help.
- I will get through it.
- I've done it before.
- It may not be so bad.

During:

- It's OK, I can cope.
- I won't take it personally.
- It'll be over soon.
- This is unpleasant, but I can get through it.
- Keep focused on the job.

After:

- It's over now.
- I got through it.
- I can talk it over with someone.
- I know what to do next time.
- Don't dwell on it – move on.

Self-calming statements (1)

Before a difficult situation

It will only last for a short while

I can ask for help

I will get through it

I've done it before

It may not be so bad

✓

Self-calming statements (2)

During a difficult situation

Self-calming statements (3)

After a difficult situation

It's over now

I got through it

I can talk it over with someone

I know what to do next time

Don't dwell on it – move on

Review 8.1

So far today we have:

- seen the benefits of using calming statements and other calm-thinking strategies to deal with our anger.

Develop personal coping statements to deal with anger

Because each of us thinks differently, remind participants that it is important for us each to develop our own set of calming statements. What works for one person may not work for someone else. Let's develop our own personal set of self-calming statements.

ACTIVITY 8.3

Ask participants to complete the 'Personal coping statements' sheet. Participants identify personal self-calming statements under the following categories:

- Before a difficult situation.

- During a difficult situation.

- After a difficult situation.

Personal coping statements

Before a difficult situation

During a difficult situation

After a difficult situation

ACTIVITY 8.4

Ask participants individually to rehearse the use of their personal calming statements for handling the difficult situation that they identified earlier (on the 'A situation when I felt angry' sheet). Ask each participant:

- What calm thinking could you do before the situation?

- What calm thinking could you do during the situation?

- What calm thinking could you do after the situation?

Summary of Session 8

Today we have:

- seen the benefits of using calming statements and other calm-thinking strategies to deal with our anger

- looked at personal coping statements for dealing with anger.

Learning to Think Calmly (3)

Aims of this session

1. Briefly review summary points from the previous session.
2. Look at some common thinking errors.
3. Explore other thinking strategies for staying calm.

Materials required

- Overhead: Common thinking errors
- 'Common thinking errors' sheet.
- Overhead: Thinking strategies.
- 'Thinking strategies' sheet.

Session plan

Briefly review summary points from the previous session

Present summary points from the previous session.

Looking at common thinking errors

Show the overhead 'Common thinking errors', and tell participants that when it comes to our thinking, many of us think about ourselves, others or situations in ways that may not be helpful or right. Many of us can make errors in our thinking. We may not see things for what they really are. Some of us may be in a habit of thinking this way.

Some of the common thinking errors people make are:

- *Thinking the worst* – expecting the worst to happen in a situation, such as thinking, 'I'm going to be thrown out of my unit,' 'They don't want me here.'

- *Taking things too personally* – thinking that every negative thing that happens is because of you, such as thinking, 'It's my fault that no one wants to watch TV in the living room,' 'It's because of me that people are unhappy.'

- *Thinking too negatively* – focusing on just the negatives and ignoring the positives of a situation, such as thinking, 'I just got invited to a party. It's because they felt sorry for me.'

- *Jumping to conclusions* – making a decision which is based on just some of the facts, such as thinking, 'They don't want me here today because yesterday I was late.'

Common thinking errors

- Thinking the worst

- Taking things personally

- Thinking too negatively

- Jumping to conclusions

ACTIVITY 9.1

As a group exercise, provide participants with the following scenario:

> Your facilitator is late for the programme. The group has been waiting 10 minutes for the programme to begin. What might be some of your thoughts?

Participants then identify the types of thoughts they may have in that situation. Within the range of responses provided, identify any of the common thinking errors: thinking the worst, taking things too personally, thinking too negatively and jumping to conclusions. Emphasise that for any situation, we may have a range of thoughts; however, some people are prone to have thoughts that contain common thinking errors.

ACTIVITY 9.2

Present participants with four situations that involve common thinking errors. As a group, participants identify and discuss the type of thinking error being displayed. Hand out the 'Common thinking errors' tip sheet to help participants identify the type of thinking error being shown. The situations are as follows:

- *Situation 1*: You are waiting for your taxi to go to the theatre with some friends. Your taxi is 5 minutes late. You think, 'I'll miss the show' (thinking the worst).

- *Situation 2*: The group had to finish off a job by the afternoon. It was not finished on time. You think, 'It's my fault' (taking things too personally).

- *Situation 3*: You have just cleaned your room, but you've forgotten to pick up your socks. You think, 'I haven't done a good job' (thinking negatively).

- *Situation 4*: You walk past your supervisor who has had a bad day. You say hello, but she doesn't say hello back. You think, 'She must be angry at me' (jumping to conclusions).

Common thinking errors

Thinking the worst

Taking things too personally

Thinking too negatively

Jumping to conclusions

Review 9.1

So far today we have:

- looked at some of the common errors people make in their thinking.

Exploring thinking strategies for staying calm

Show the overhead 'Thinking strategies', and emphasise there are thinking strategies that help you to feel calm. We can use these strategies for dealing with anger.

- *Distract yourself* – sometimes dwelling on things can make us feel angrier. Thinking of something else can help us to feel better. It can give us a break from negative feelings and we can come back and deal better with the situation some time later. We can distract ourselves by counting to 10, thinking of a relaxing scene or thinking of something that gives us a good feeling.

- *Look at the funny side of a situation* – trying to see the funny side of a situation may help us to feel better. When we have funny thoughts, we can't feel angry. This helps us to see the situation less seriously.

- *Praise yourself for positive efforts* – even if we are left with negative feelings after the situation, praising ourselves for our effort to stay in control is good. It can help us to cope better next time.

- *Focus on the task* – keep focused on the job, rather than your feelings of anger.

Thinking strategies

- **Distract yourself**

- **Use humour**

- **Praise youself**

- **Keep focused on the job**

ACTIVITY 9.3

Ask participants to role-play a situation using a range of alternative thinking strategies. Set the following scene:

> You live in a home with a number of other people. You are busy washing the dishes when suddenly one of the people you live with says to you, 'I hate living with you.'

Participants are supported to role-play the following alternative thinking responses:

- *Distraction*: Thinks about something nice to do later on in the day.

- *Humour*: Thinks 'I'm glad he doesn't say that every day!'

- *Self-praise*: Thinks 'I have done a good job in trying to stay calm.'

- *Focusing on the task*: Thinks 'just get on with the job – washing the dishes.'

ACTIVITY 9.4

Ask participants to complete the 'Thinking strategies' sheet. Participants identify a range of alternative calm-thinking strategies they can use personally, under the following categories:

- *Distraction* (one way of distracting yourself).

- *Humour* (one thing which you could think to yourself to make light of the situation).

- *Self-praise* (one thing you could say to yourself to reinforce your effort).

- *Focusing on the task* (one thing you could say to yourself to keep you focused on what you are doing).

Thinking strategies

Distracting myself

_____

_____

Using humour

_____

_____

Praising myself for effort

_____

_____

Keeping focused on the job

_____

_____

Summary of Session 9

Today we have:

- looked at some of the common errors people make in their thinking

- looked at other calm-thinking strategies.

Session 10

Learning to Handle Problems

Aims of this session

1. Briefly review summary points from the previous session.
2. Identify the sorts of problems we can experience and how they can impact on our anger.
3. Discuss problem-solving strategies.
4. Explore personal problem-solving strategies.

Materials required

- Whiteboard (optional).
- Overhead: Problem-solving tips.
- 'Problem-solving tips' sheet.
- 'Problem scenario' sheets.
- 'Personal problem-solving' sheet.

Session plan

Briefly review summary points from the previous session

Present summary points from the previous session.

Identify the sorts of problems we can experience and how they can impact on our anger

Ask participants what is meant by *problems*. Emphasise that problems are the difficulties we face in our day-to-day lives. We can face problems at home, at work and at services we use. We can face problems with family members, friends, people we know and people in the community. Problems are a normal part of life; everyone experiences problems at certain times. Ask participants whether they know anyone who has never had a problem in their life. Obviously, the answer here is 'No'.

Emphasise that all of us experience problems from time to time. When some people experience problems, this can lead to feelings of anger. For example, we are waiting for a taxi to get somewhere and the taxi is late. This may be a problem for someone and they may start to feel angry.

ACTIVITY 10.1

As a group activity, identify and discuss a problem each participant has experienced and how it affected the way they felt. Emphasise that each of us experiences problems from time to time, and that experiencing some problems is a normal part of life. Emphasise that when we have a problem, we may feel angry.

> **Review 10.1**
>
> So far today we have:
>
> - talked about problems. We said everyone experiences problems. Sometimes having problems can lead to feelings of anger.

Discuss problem-solving strategies

Show the overhead 'Problem-solving tips', and say to participants, when we face a problem, it is often helpful to try to solve it. There are a number of steps we can take to try to solve the problems we face. These steps are:

- *Find out what the problem is.* Be clear about the problem and what is happening in the situation you are faced with.

- *Think about some of the things you can do to solve the problem.* Usually there are many choices you can make.

- *From all these choices, work out which one is the best.* Choose the thing that will help you to get what you want without causing any further problems for you or others.

- *Try it out and see how it goes.* If it works, continue with it. If it does not, then try another way of solving the problem.

Hand out the 'Problem-solving tips' sheet and use this sheet to reinforce the above points.

Problem-solving tips

- Find out what the problem is

- Think about some things you can do to solve the problem

- From all these choices, work out which one is best

- Try it and see

Problem-solving tips

Find out what the problem is

Think about some things you can do to solve the problem

From all these choices, work out which is best

Try it and see how it goes

ACTIVITY 10.2

Use the situations in the 'Problem scenario' sheets to explore specific problem-solving strategies. The situations in the 'Problem scenario' sheets are summarised below. Note that responses for this activity can be entered on a whiteboard.

Problem scenarios:

- You are upset about something. You want to talk to a staff person about it in private. A person you live with listens in to the conversation. You get angry.

- A person is rude to your friend. He calls your friend a degrading name. You get angry.

- You are in a queue to get lunch. Another person pushes in front of you. You get angry.

Problem-solving steps:

- What is the problem?

- What are some solutions?

- Which is the best solution?

- Try it and see…

Problem scenario (1)

You are upset about something

You want to talk to a staff person about it in private

A person you live with listens in to the conversation

You get angry

Problem scenario (2)

A person is rude to your friend

He calls your friend names

You get angry

Problem scenario (3)

You are in a queue to get lunch

Another person pushes in front of you

You get angry

> **Review 10.2**
>
> So far today we have:
>
> - talked about problems
> - talked about some steps we can use to solve problems. This was to show us a helpful way of handling problems.

Explore personal problem-solving strategies

Tell participants that when we feel angry, this usually means that there is a problem that we need to look at. Many of the problems that we are faced with can be solved. If we are calm and relaxed, we may be able to think it through and find a solution. Each of us deals with our problems in our own way. Let's look at how each of us tends to deal with problems. Also, let's look at how each of us can deal with problems in a better way.

ACTIVITY 10.3

Ask participants to complete the 'Personal problem-solving' sheet, indicating a problem situation where they felt angry and what they did in that circumstance. Ask participants to indicate an alternative problem-solving strategy that they could have used in this circumstance, and could use in similar circumstances in the future.

Personal problem-solving

What is a problem situation where I felt angry?

_____

_____

What did I do in this situation?

_____

_____

How could I have handled this better?

_____

_____

Summary of Session 10

Today we have:

- talked about problems.

- talked about some steps we can use to solve problems. This was to show us a helpful way of handling problems.

- looked at how we solve problems, and some better ways of solving problems in the future.

Learning to Speak Up for Ourselves

Aims of this session

1. Briefly review summary points from the previous session.

2. Explore why being assertive is important for anger management.

3. Highlight the differences between passive, aggressive and assertive behaviour styles.

4. Explore techniques for assertive behaviour.

5. Identify situations in which participants behave aggressively and ways participants can be more assertive in these situations.

Materials required

*   Overhead: Being assertive can help us.

*   Overhead: Passive, aggressive, assertive styles.

*   'Passive, aggressive, assertive' cards.

*   'Situation' cards.

*   Overhead: Assertive behaviour tips.

*   'Assertive behaviour tips' sheet.

*   'Less aggressive – more assertive' sheet.

Session plan

Briefly review summary points from the previous session

Present summary points from the previous session.

Explore why being assertive is important for anger management

Ask participants what it means to be assertive. Emphasise that being assertive means to stand up for yourself, your rights and your beliefs in a responsible way. We will discuss this in more detail later. Ask participants why being assertive is important for dealing with angry feelings.

Show the overhead 'Being assertive can help us', and emphasise that being assertive can help us manage our anger better:

- It's a good way of communicating our thoughts and feelings.

- We avoid getting too angry.

- It gives us a greater sense of control in our lives.

- We can feel better within ourselves.

- It can give us more self-confidence.

- We are less likely to experience negative consequences.

Being assertive can help us

- communicate our thoughts
- avoid getting too angry
- gives us greater control
- we can feel better within ourselves
- gives us more confidence
- less negative consequences

Review 11.1

So far today we have:

- talked about how being assertive can help us manage our anger better.

Highlight the differences between passive, aggressive and assertive behaviour styles

Show the overhead 'Passive, aggressive, assertive styles', and remind participants that in living and communicating with others, we behave in many different ways. Sometimes we fail to speak up. An example of this is when we don't say 'No' to people when we really feel like saying 'No'. This means we keep our feelings bottled up. This sort of behaviour is known as being 'passive' or being 'meek'.

Sometimes we feel that the only way to express ourselves is through getting really angry. An example of this is when we yell at other people when we want something. This can make others feel awful, and as if they have been treated unfairly by our anger outburst. This sort of behaviour is known as being 'aggressive' or 'pushy'.

But there is another way we can express ourselves, without being passive or aggressive. This is known as being 'assertive'. When we are assertive, we speak up for ourselves, but in a way that is fair to us and fair to others. An example of assertive behaviour is when we say 'No' to people when we feel like saying 'No'. Another example of assertive behaviour is letting someone know we want something while staying calm and not getting really angry. It is important to say that it is generally good to be assertive when we need to be. But there are also some times in life when we may choose *not* to be assertive. For example, you may choose not to speak up about something that is not too important or that might hurt someone's feelings, as long as you are making the decision and are in control.

Passive, aggressive, assertive styles

**Passive
(Meek)**

**Aggressive
(Pushy)**

**Assertive
(Speaking up)**

ACTIVITY 11.1

Present 'problem' scenario (see below). Role-play passive, aggressive and assertive behaviour responses to this scenario. The participants use the 'Passive, aggressive, assertive' cards (which need to be cut out as indicated) to indicate which response style you are displaying. The problem situation is as follows:

A shopkeeper gives you the wrong change – he has given you less change than he should have.

- *Passive response style*: Does not say anything, and walks away.

- *Aggressive response style*: Starts yelling, 'How dare you give me the wrong change, you are a fool. Give me the right change now!'

- *Assertive response style*: Calmly says, 'Excuse me, you gave me the wrong amount of change. Please give me the right change.'

Passive, aggressive, assertive cards

Passive (Meek)

Aggressive (Pushy)

Assertive (Speaking up)

We will now do another activity to help us better understand the differences between passive, aggressive and assertive behaviour.

ACTIVITY 11.2

Ask participants to role-play one of three interpersonal situations involving either a passive, aggressive or assertive response style. One participant at a time selects a 'Situation' card and is facilitated to role-play the scenario represented on this card. The other participants are asked to judge which style of behaviour is being used. Participants indicate their judgement by using the 'Passive, aggressive, assertive cards'.

Interpersonal Situation	Response	Response style
You are sitting on the couch. Someone says, 'Get off – I want to sit there.'	You get off, and don't speak up.	Passive
Your house-mate makes a mess.	You say, 'You're an idiot. Clean up or move out.'	Aggressive
Someone touches your body. You don't like it.	You say, 'Don't touch me.'	Assertive

Passive situation card

You are sitting on a couch

Someone says, 'Get off! I want to sit there!'

You get off and don't speak up

Aggressive situation card

Your house-mate makes a mess

You say, 'You're an idiot. Clean up or move out!'

Assertive situation card

Someone touches your body

You don't like it

You say, 'Don't touch me!'

Review 11.2

So far today we have:

- talked about how being assertive can help us manage our anger better.

- talked about the differences between passive, aggressive and assertive behaviour. We learnt about three different ways people can behave in situations.

Explore techniques for assertive behaviour

Show the overhead 'Assertive behaviour tips', and ask participants how we show we are assertive. Emphasise that we:

- look at the person

- tell people what we want or what we don't want, using our voice or another form of communication

- sit or stand up straight

- use gestures.

All these things let others know what we want or what we don't want. Hand out the 'Assertive behaviour tips' sheet and emphasise these points.

Assertive behaviour tips

- Look at the person

- Tell people what you want or don't want

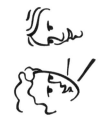

- Sit or stand up straight

- Use gestures

Assertive behaviour tips

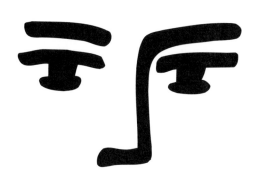

Look at the person

Tell people what you want or what you don't want

Sit or stand up straight

Use gestures

Review 11.3

Today we have:

- talked about how being assertive can help us manage our anger better

- talked about the differences between passive, aggressive and assertive behaviour

- talked about assertive behaviour and seen some examples of people being assertive. This is to help us learn more about what being assertive means.

Identify situations in which participants behave aggressively and ways partici-pants can be more assertive in these situations

For some of us, there may be situations where we behave aggressively or pushily. We will now complete an activity that will help us look at our own behaviour, and help us work out in which situations we behave aggressively. We will also look at ways we can be less aggressive and more assertive in these situations.

ACTIVITY 11.3

Ask participants to complete the 'Less aggressive – more assertive' sheet as a group. Participants provide responses to the questions: 'In what situation can I be less aggressive?', 'How can I be more assertive in these situations?', and 'Who will support me if I need help?' This is a potential area for the participants to follow up in collaboration with their support people.

Less aggressive – more assertive

In what situations can I be less aggressive?

_____

_____

How can I be more assertive in these situations?

_____

_____

Who will support me if I need help?

_____

_____

Summary of Session 11

Today we have:

- talked about how being assertive can help us manage our anger better

- talked about the differences between passive, aggressive and assertive behaviour

- talked about assertive behaviour, and saw some examples of people being assertive

- looked at situations where each of us do and don't behave assertively

- looked at ways we can each behave more assertively. This is so we can have more control of our own lives.

Session 12
Putting it all Together

Aims of this session

1. Briefly review the summary points from the previous session.
2. Provide an overview of information covered in the sessions.
3. Develop a personal anger management plan.
4. Evaluate skills developed and identify any areas of continued need.

Materials required

*   'Personal anger management plan' sheet.
*   'Anger management evaluation' sheet.
*   Certificate.

Session plan

Briefly review summary points from the previous session

> Present summary points from the previous session.

Provide an overview of information covered in the sessions

> Emphasise to the participants that over the sessions we have talked about anger and better ways of dealing with anger. We talked about:

> *   an introduction to anger management
> *   recognising feelings and anger
> *   helpful and unhelpful ways of dealing with anger
> *   learning to relax
> *   learning to think calmly
> *   learning to speak up for ourselves
> *   learning to handle problems.

ACTIVITY 12.1

Ask participants to recall one key point from these sessions that they felt was important to them.

> **Review 12.1**
>
> So far today we have:
>
> - gone over the information we covered in all the sessions.

Develop a personal anger management plan

Suggest to the participants that we put together some of the things that we've learnt over the sessions. We will now develop a personal plan for dealing better with our anger.

ACTIVITY 12.2

Ask participants to complete the 'Personal anger management plan'. This sheet provides a summary of strategies the person can use for managing their anger more effectively, from the range of strategies discussed over the course of the programme. For example, a particular person may choose to adopt the following strategies:

- Use muscle relaxation.
- Use the statement, 'I can get through this.'
- Distract myself.
- Try to solve the problem.

As well, further learning and skill development could be followed up. For example:

- Learn more about relaxation.
- Develop new interests and hobbies.

This is an important summary document that the participants can use as a quick reference for managing their anger. Consider having the document laminated and returned to the participants, who can then place the sheet in an easy-to-access location.

Personal anger management plan

Strategies I can use to deal with anger better...

_____

_____

_____

_____

Areas I need to learn about...

_____

_____

_____

_____

> **Review 12.2**
>
> So far today we have:
>
> - gone over the information we covered in all the sessions
> - developed a personal plan for managing anger better.

Evaluate skills developed and identify any areas of continued need

We will now look at what we've learnt over the sessions, and which areas we feel we still need to work on.

ACTIVITY 12.3

Ask participants to complete the 'Anger management evaluation' sheet. Participants should tick 'Yes' for areas where they feel their knowledge/skills have developed since commencing the course, and 'Needs more work' for areas where they feel that their knowledge/skills need to be developed further. Participants then come together and discuss their responses.

Use this opportunity to:

- reflect and recap on the specific skills covered in the course (for example, 'So, who remembers what we learnt when we talked about feelings?')

- explore instances of skill acquisition (for example, 'Who feels they now know more about feelings?') and acknowledge this positive progress

- explore areas of continued need (for example, 'Who feels they still need to learn more about feelings?') and specific follow-up to address these needs. This is a potential area for participants to follow up in collaboration with their support people.

Anger management evaluation sheet

Session	Area	Yes	Needs more work
Introduction to Anger Management	I understand what anger is.		
Learning about Feelings and Anger	I know about different feelings.		
	I know about the situations in which I feel angry.		
	I know about the changes (e.g. bodily changes) I experience when angry.		
Learning about Helpful and Unhelpful Ways of Dealing with Anger	I know about helpful ways of dealing with anger.		
Learning to Relax	I know about different ways of relaxing.		
	I know how to use relaxation.		
Learning to Think Calmly	I know about the difference between calm thoughts and angry thoughts.		
	I know how to use calm thinking.		
Learning to Handle Problems	I know some helpful ways of solving problems.		
Learning to Speak Up for Ourselves	I know how to speak up for myself, without becoming angry.		
Putting it all Together	I have developed a personal anger management plan.		

ACTIVITY 12.4

Participants are individually presented with their certificates.

ACTIVITY 12.4

Anger management programme certificate

Name

has completed the anger management programme

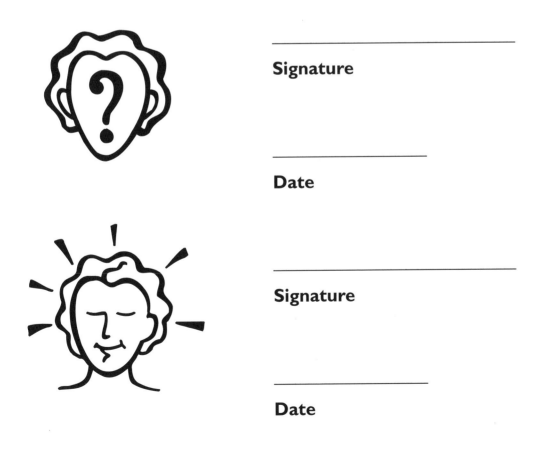

Signature

Date

Signature

Date

Summary of Session 12

Today we have:

- gone over the information we covered in all the sessions

- developed a personal plan for managing anger better

- looked at the sorts of things we learnt and the sorts of things we can continue to work on.

References

Benson, B.A. (1992) *Teaching Anger Management to Persons with Mental Retardation.* Worthington, OH: IDS Publishing.

Hill, B.K. and Bruininks, R.H. (1984) 'Maladaptive behavior of mentally retarded individuals in residential facilities.' *American Journal of Mental Deficiency 88,* 380–7.

Howells, P.M., Rogers, C. and Wilcock, S. (2000) 'Evaluating a cognitive/behavioural approach to anger management skills to adults with learning disabilities.' *British Journal of Learning Disabilities 28,* 137–42.

King, N., Lancaster, N., Wynne, G., Nettleton, N. and Davis, R. (1999) 'Cognitive-behavioural anger management training for adults with mild intellectual disability.' *Scandinavian Journal of Behaviour Therapy 28,* 19–22.

McVilly, K.R. (2002) *Positive Behaviour Support for People with Intellectual Disability: Evidence-based Practice, Promoting Quality of Life.* Sydney: Australian Society for the Study of Intellectual Disability Inc.

Novaco, R.W. (1975) *Anger Control: The Development and Evaluation of an Experimental Treatment.* Lexington, MA: Heath.

Sigafoos, J., Elkins, J., Kerr, M. and Attwood, T. (1994) 'A survey of aggressive behavior among a population of persons with intellectual disability in Queensland.' *Journal of Intellectual Disability Research 38,* 369–81.

Smith, S., Branford, D., Collacott, R.A., Cooper, S.A. and McGrother, C. (1996) 'Prevalence and cluster typology of maladaptive behaviours in a geographically defined population of adults with learning disabilities.' *British Journal of Psychiatry 169,* 219–27.

Taylor, J.L. (2002) 'A review of assessment and treatment of anger and aggression in offenders with intellectual disability.' *Journal of Intellectual Disability Research 46,* 57–73.

Taylor, J.L., Novaco, R.W., Gillmer, B. and Thorne, I. (2002) 'Cognitive-behavioural treatment of anger intensity in offenders with intellectual disabilities.' *Journal of Applied Research in Intellectual Disabilities 15,* 151–65.